DON'T GO OUT IN YOUR UNDERWEAR!

Poems by Babs Bell Hajdusiewicz ✳ Illustrations by Elizabeth Sawyer

 Dominie Press, Inc.

Publisher: Raymond Yuen
Illustrator: Elizabeth Sawyer
Editorial Assistant: Bob Rowland
Designer: Michael Khoury

Published by:

🔂 **Dominie Press, Inc.**

1949 Kellogg Avenue
Carlsbad, CA 92008

ISBN 1-56270-802-3
Printed in Singapore by PH Productions Pte Ltd

3 4 5 6 7 8 9 IP 04 03 02 01 00

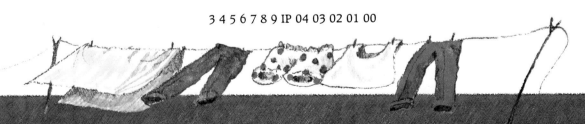

✳ Table of Contents ✳

To Jerry, Nick & Alison

AND

to all my language-loving friends

I,
Myself,
& Me

I Like Me!

This morning, I stood up and said:

I like myself from toes to head!
I like the way I look today!
I like the way I work and play!
I like the way I act with friends!
I like the way my body bends!
I like who I was born to be!
I like myself!
    Hey!
        I like ME!

I Can!

I can count.
I can hop.
I can use a broom and mop.
I can dance.
I can draw.
I can build things with a saw.
I can wink.
I can think.
I can clean the bathroom sink.
I can read.
I can sing.
I can do most anything!

My Faces

I can make . . .
a funny face
a sunny face
a twitchy-nose-like-bunny face
a pouting face
a shouting face
a wondering-and-doubting face
a sad face
a mad face
a feeling-kinda-bad face
a scary face
a merry face
a what-a-sour-berry! face

Whatever face you see in place
is my how-I-am-feeling face!

Special Me

Lots of people have two eyes
two ears
one mouth
one nose
two thighs.

But no one else has MY two eyes
MY ears
MY mouth
MY nose
MY thighs!

Lots ot people have two wrists
two arms
one neck
one chin
two fists.

But no one else has MY two wrists
MY arms
MY neck
MY chin
MY fists!

I'm Special Me
One–of–a–kind!
Another ME you'll never find!

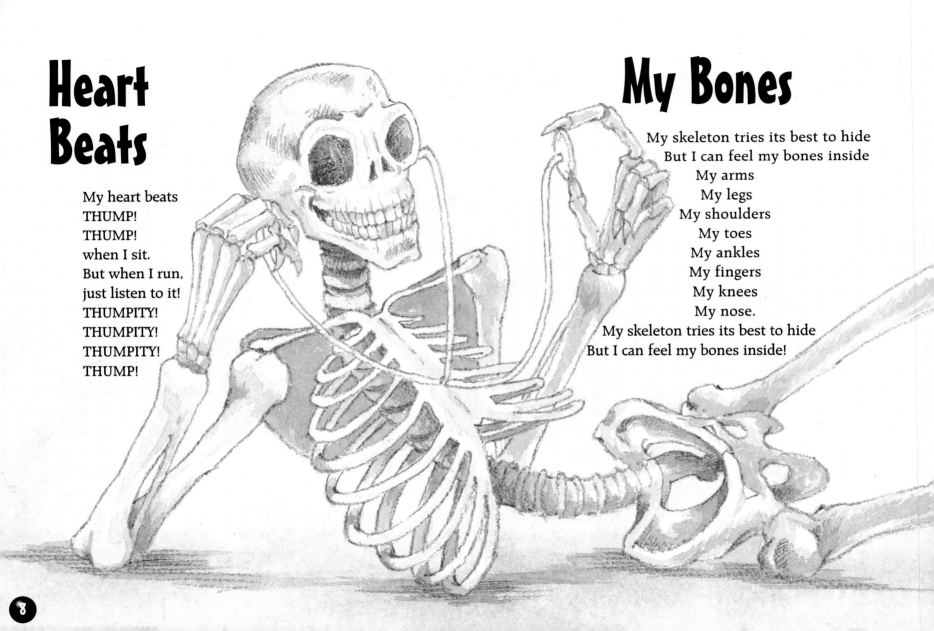

Heart Beats

My heart beats
THUMP!
THUMP!
when I sit.
But when I run,
just listen to it!
THUMPITY!
THUMPITY!
THUMPITY!
THUMP!

My Bones

My skeleton tries its best to hide
But I can feel my bones inside
My arms
My legs
My shoulders
My toes
My ankles
My fingers
My knees
My nose.
My skeleton tries its best to hide
But I can feel my bones inside!

I, Myself, & Me

If I come in and no one's home,
  I tell myself that I
Am really not so all alone—
  There's Me, Myself, and I.

"Me," I say, "what shall we do?"
  "Let's ask Myself," says Me.
Myself and I, we then sit down
  To make a plan with Me.

But just about the time that we,
  (That's I, Myself, and Me)
Get all our talking sorted out,
  In comes my family!

Bed Rest

An animal rests
in a pen
or a nest
or a den
or a river
or sea.

But I like to rest
in a bed
and it's best . . .
if Teddy is resting with me.

9

Me a Mess?

Unclean and unbuckled,
Unfastened, untied,
Unfit to be seen,
I'm undignified.
Unfolded, unbuttoned,
Unbecoming, no less.
Unfortunately, I'm
Unaware I'm a mess.

I Did It!

I tried
and tried
and tried
and tried
and then I quit
and cried.
I cried
and cried
and cried
and cried
and then I quit
and tried
and
I did it!

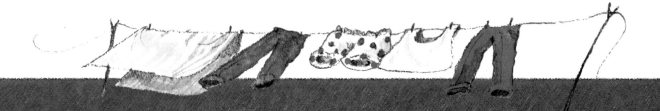

My Turn

My hand went up. I wanted to say
the funniest thing that had happened today.
I waited and waited and waited until
the others were finished, and all was still.

But when they were finished—
Oh, golly!
Oh, gee!
I couldn't remember what had happened to me!

When I Grow Up

When I grow up, who will I be
besides the person who is ME?
I might bring mail.
I might play drums.
I might drive trucks.
I might grow plums.
I might fight fires.
I might trim trees.
I might type letters.
I might fix knees.

When I grow up, I think I'll be
a worker who works, but I'll still be ME!

It's Not My Fault!

I try my best to be polite.
I know what's wrong and what is right.
But sometimes little parts of me
"act up" and "bug" my family.

My tongue sticks out.
My knuckles crunch.
My lips make smacking sounds at lunch.
My fingers poke and pinch and pick.
My feet jump out and trip or kick.
My mouth says words that aren't nice—
Today it spit . . . and tattled—twice!

It's not my fault that parts of me
act rude and "bug" my family!
So don't blame me for what they did!
It's not my fault! I'm just a kid!

The
Truth

A Ruff Day

I don't believe what I just saw—
Sam whacked Maggie in the jaw!
Maggie bit her brother's nose,
and Gigi pounced on Maggie's toes!
Then Elmer sneaked up—
    that's not kind!
He sank his teeth in Sam's behind!
And Maggie led the next attack
to land with Sam on Elmer's back!
Then Gigi sprawled atop the heap,
and all four puppies fell asleep!

The Truth

Toby says that I should run—
"No one will know you threw it."
Toby says that I should lie—
"Just say you didn't do it."

But Daddy says to tell the truth
and never, ever lie.
So I'll tell them I threw the ball
but, first—I'm gonna cry.

Vinny's My Friend

I forgot to bring my lunch
but Vinny had lots—
he gave me a bunch
of grapes
and a cracker
and even the end
of a pickle he had—
Vinny's my friend!

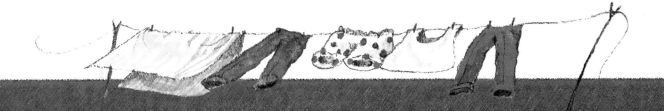

It's a Fact!

It's easy to spot them.
  Their manners are rude.
They talk while they're chewing
  whole mouthfuls of food.

It's easy to spot them.
  They don't like to share.
They interrupt others.
  They brag and they swear.

It's easy to spot them.
  They never say, "Thanks."
They never say, "Sorry!"
  for meanness or pranks.

It's easy to spot them.
  They cut in a line.
They grab things from others
  with "Gimme! That's mine!"

It's easy to spot them—
  the way the Rudes act
is gross and disgusting
  and rude—it's a fact!

The Beach

This is the beach that time made.

This is the sand
That covers the beach that time made.

These are the rocks
That crumble to sand
That covers the beach that time made.

These are the waves
That beat the rocks
That crumble to sand
That covers the beach that time made.

This is the sea
That holds the waves
That beat the rocks
That crumble to sand
That covers the beach that time made.

This is the moon
That rocks the sea
That holds the waves
That beat the rocks
That crumble to sand
That covers the beach that time made.

Gramps & I

Gramps and I rocked on the porch one night.
Saw a strange little light in the dark dark night.
We looked to the left.
And we looked to the right.
'Twas nothing but a firefly glowing in the night.

Gramps and I rocked on the porch one night.
Heard a strange little noise in the dark dark night.
We listened to the left.
And we listened to the right.
'Twas nothing but a screen door closing in the night.

Gramps and I rocked on the porch one night.
Smelled a strange little smell in the dark dark night.
We sniffed to the left.
And we sniffed to the right.
'Twas nothing but a tailpipe coughing in the night.

Gramps and I rocked on the porch one night.
And I heard a noise in the dark dark night.
I listened to the left.
And I listened to the right.
'Twas nothing but my grandpa snoring in the night.

A Mighty Knight

In the daytime,
  a mighty knight
  fights mighty fights in the sunlight.
At nighttime,
  the mighty knight
  fights mighty fights by flashlight.
But at midnight,
  a mighty frightened knight
  goes nighty-night
  with a nightlight.

Dragon Guest

A dragon guest can be a pest
  Unless, as host, you do your best
  To serve the beast a feast of roast,
  two-thousand eggs, two tons of toast.

Then give your guest some time to rest—
Suggest he let his food digest.
And while he rests, you tiptoe past
Or Dragon Guest will be your last!

It's Okay to Disagree

I love Sis and Sis loves me,
but sometimes we do not agree.

Sis said, "Let me hold your bear."
But I said, "I don't want to share!"
Sis said, "Don't turn on that light!"
But I said, "I'm afraid at night!"

Sis and I tried not to fight—
I shared my bear.
I got a light.
I love Sis and Sis loves me.
And it's okay to disagree.

Alas!

Jack and Jill
Went up the hill
To fetch a pail of water.
Jack fell down
And broke his crown,
But, alas!
Jill was wearing her seat belt!

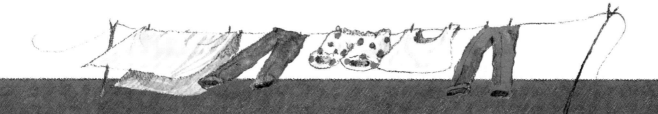

Bunny Rabbit's Predicament

Come along and meet Bunny!
He's a wee little rabbit
Who once upon a time, had a strange kind of habit.
He adored chewing gum from morning till night
And he often blew bubbles to his own delight.

But one day he blew a gum bubble so big
It popped, leaving Bunny with a thingamujig
Stuck to his whiskers, his nose, and his chin—
'Twas an awkward predicament Bunny was in!

Well, he squirmed
And he wiggled
And he snorted
And he sniffed
And he blew his gummy nose in his handkerchief.

And wouldn't you know, that hankie held tight.
It dangled from his nose like a parasite
Which caused Bunny's nose to begin to itch
And the itching caused the whiskers on Bunny to twitch.

Well, he squirmed
And he wiggled
And he snorted
And he sniffed
But his nose was still fastened to the handkerchief.

Then along came a chum with a cupful of ice
Which he offered to the rabbit with some gummy advice:
"Your predicament is sticky but the gum will come off.
All we need is more ice from the watering trough."

"My, my, that's peculiar," said Bunny with a sigh,
"But my friend's here to help, so it can't hurt to try."
Then off hopped the rabbit and his chum to the trough.
Got the ice, froze the gum, and the hankie dropped off.

Now, the moral of the tale is "Never despair."
An unsolvable problem is generally rare.
Though you may need some help to get a job done,
'Cause two heads are sometimes better than one!

My True Story

When I tell my true story to you,
you'll prob'ly say, "That can't be true!"

My head fell off the other day.
  "That can't be true!"
My head fell off and rolled away.
  "That can't be true!"
So I went shopping for a head.
  "That can't be true!"
"We've lots of heads," the store clerk said.
  "That can't be true!"
Then I picked out a head to buy.
  "That can't be true!"
But that head's price was much too high!
  "That can't be true!"
I headed home without a head.
  "That can't be true!"
And there was my head—in my bed!
  "That can't be true!"
My head began to squeal and scream!
  "That can't be true!"
That noise woke me from my bad dream!

 "That <u>CAN</u> be true!"

In the
Middle

In & Out

Momma Skunk had baby skunks.
She named them In and Out.
One day she shooed them out to play,
"Go out now, In and Out!"

"And, Out, stay out and don't come in
Without your brother, In.
If you get tired of playing out,
Come in, but bring In in."

But In, who liked to play small tricks,
Hid out while Out went out.
And Momma Skunk was unaware
That only Out was out.

When moments later, Out appeared
Inside to search for In,
Momma Skunk admonished Out,
"You were to bring In in!"

"But, Momma, In did not go out,"
Said Out to Momma Skunk.
"My, my!" said Momma, "Can In be
Asleep in his top bunk?"

When In was not upon his bed,
Out ran outside to see
If In had sneaked out...sure enough!
Out found him easily.

"Oh, Out, how did you find our In?
You're quicker than two winks!"
"'Twas easy, Momma, surely you
Remember our In-stincts!"

Squirmy Earthworm

to the tune of "EENSY WEENSY SPIDER"

Squirmy, Squirmy Earthworm
Lives down in the ground.
But watch her wiggle out
When rain falls all around!

Squirmy, Squirmy Earthworm
Squirms along the ground.
But watch her disappear when
Blackbirds come around!

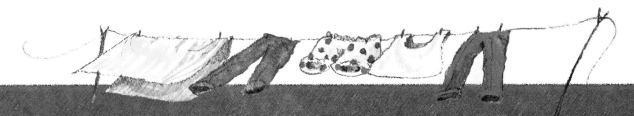

Charlie's Chickens

Charlie Chip was hungry
For some chunky chicken soup
So he went to choose a chicken
From his champion chicken coop.

But Charlie's champion chickens
Charmed poor Charlie with a chant,
"You can't make champions into chunks!
You can't!
You can't!
You can't!"

So Charlie Chip serves chitlins
With chilled chunks of cheddar cheese
While his charming champion chickens chant,
"Charlie, pass the peas!"

Gobble! Gobble! Munch!

Gobble, gobble, munch!
Gobble, gobble, munch!
What will you be serving
on your street for lunch?

Don't serve me paper!
Don't serve me cans!
Don't serve me metal
or aluminum pans!

Don't serve me plastic!
Don't serve me glass!
I would rather munch on
egg shells or grass.

Gobble, gobble, munch!
Gobble, gobble, munch!
What will you be serving
this garbage truck for lunch?

Lining Up

If I am first,
then you can't be
unless you stand in front of me.
Then I am second.
I'm behind
the one who brags, "I'm first in line!"

If others come to join our line,
one person's third
and stands behind.
Then fourth is next
and fifth is last—
Unless we all turn
around real fast!

POP! POPPITY! POP!

POP! POPPITY! POP!
POP! POPPITY! POP!
Pop, poppity, popcorn popped and popped!
So I got a bowl and filled it up.
But the POP! POPPITY! POP! POP!
did not stop.
So I got a tub and filled it up.
But the POP! POPPITY! POP! POP!
did not stop.
So I got a truck and filled it up.
But the POP! POPPITY! POP! POP!
did not stop.
So I found the switch and turned it off.
And the POP!
POPPITY!
POP!
POP!
popped
and stopped!

Six Speckled Hens

Six speckled hens
build six straw nests.
Busy, Busy, Busy!
Busy, Busy, Busy!

Six speckled hens
lay six brown eggs.
Cluck, Cluck, Cluck!
Cluck, Cluck, Cluck!

Six speckled hens
warm six brown eggs.
Shhh, Shhh, Shhh!
Shhh, Shhh, Shhh!

Six sharp bills
tap six brown eggs.
Peck, Peck, Peck!
Peck, Peck, Peck!

Six baby chicks
break six brown eggs.
Crack, Crack, Crack!
Crack, Crack, Crack!

Six baby chicks
leave six broken shells.
Wobble, Wobble, Wobble!
Wobble, Wobble, Wobble!

Six speckled hens
find six wiggly worms.
Tug, Tug, Tug!
Tug, Tug, Tug!

Six hungry chicks
eat six wiggly worms.
Gobble, Gobble, Gobble!
Gobble, Gobble, Gobble!

Six sleepy chicks
take six quiet naps.
Zzzz, Zzzz, Zzzz!
Zzzz, Zzzz, Zzzz!

In the Middle

Being in the middle
sometimes means security,
though sometimes "in the middle"
is an ugly place to be.

I like it in the middle
when a friend's on either side.
I like it in the middle
on a roller coaster ride.

It's perfect in the middle
of the summer out of school.
So's diving to the middle
of a big ol' swimming pool.

I like it in the middle,
not the first
but not the last.
And the middle's great for looking
at the future
and the past.

But being in the middle
isn't any fun for me
when my parents start to argue
and I have to referee.

And in the middle's scary
those few minutes when we're stuck
going sixty miles per hour
smacked between two semi-trucks.

I hate it in the middle
of a long suspension bridge,
but the middle of the week is worse—
there's nothing in the fridge!

And being in the middle
isn't any kind of treat,
when my sister and my brother
are the bread
and I'm the meat.

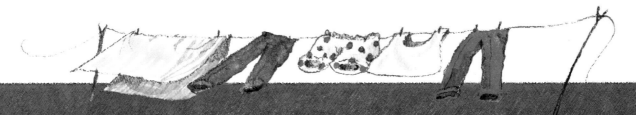

Let's Talk!

Let's not kick or hit or fight.
Let's find a way
to make this right.

When you and I do not agree,
I'll talk to you.
You talk to me.

Lost and ~~Not~~ Found

My Mom (she's on a diet)
says she's lost another pound.
I've tried to help her find it,
but it's nowhere to be found.

Subway

Down
Down
Down
Down
Under the ground.
Rumble
Rumble
Rumble
Rumble
What's that sound?
Whoosh-a
Rumble
Whoosh-a
Rumble
Zoom
Zoom
Zoom
The subway train is zooming
through its underground room.

On Halloween

I go up and down the street
on Halloween,
I say "BOO!"
and "TRICK or TREAT!"
on Halloween.
I scare everyone I meet
on Halloween.
Then I come home
and eat my treats
on Halloween!

Who-o-o-o-o Am I?

Who-o-o-o-o am I
who shakes new blossoms off the trees?
Who-o-o-o-o am I
who snatches hats off heads with ease?
Who-o-o-o-o am I
who chases litter down the street?
Who-o-o-o-o am I
who tries to whip you off your feet?
Who-o-o-o-o am I
who lifts dry leaves on autumn days?
Who-o-o-o-o am I
who helps the moon make ocean waves?
Who-o-o-o-o am I
who shows the bushes how to dance?
Who-o-o-o-o am I
who dries your dripping shirts and pants?
I am the wind—
That's who-o-o-o-o-o-o!

Under Outer

Under Outer

I wear my underwear
   next to my skin.
And my outerwear on top
   to keep my underwear in.

All Gone!

Our baby likes the laundry chute—
He plays "all gone!"
           It's kinda cute.

His shoes and socks go down the chute.
His jeans and shirt go down the chute.
His underwear goes down the chute.
And then . . . he's in his birthday suit!

Baby Brother

He sucks and sucks
and wets his diaper.
Then he grunts
and needs a wiper.

So it goes with Baby Brother—
In one end and out the other.

Silly Trees

I'm glad I'm me, and not a tree!
Some trees and I, we don't agree
On how to dress and what to wear
Upon our limbs and in our hair.

In summertime when it is hot,
Those trees wear all the clothes they've got.
And then in winter's ice and snow,
They stand there nude from head to toe!

The Girl's Room?

I know each sign
  and what it means,
but does it change
  when I wear jeans?

Doing Business

My daddy's on the phone right now.
He says he's almost done.
My daddy's doing business
with a man in Washington.

My mother's doing business, too.
She's not at home today.
My mother's doing business
at her office far away.

And I'll be doing business
with our brand new pooper-scoop,
'cause my puppy's doing business
on our newly-painted stoop.

Don't Go Out in Your Underwear!

If you went out in your underwear,
they might fall down—
then you'd be bare!
And if you went out in your underwear,
people might laugh
and point and stare!
And if you went out in your underwear,
you might get a cold
and sneeze
and cough
and even freeze your bottom off!
And then . . .
Where would you wear your underwear?

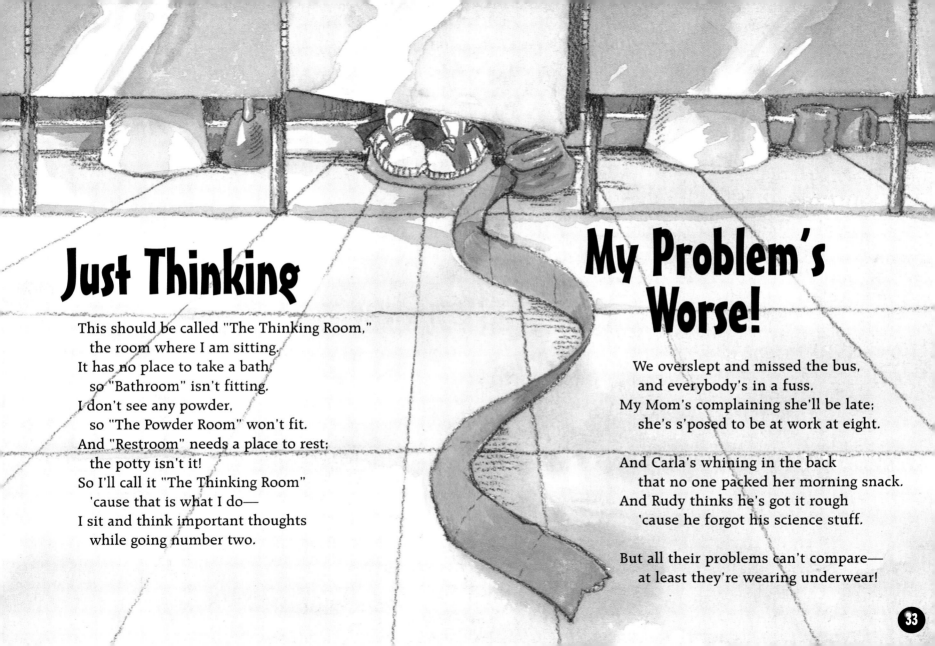

Just Thinking

This should be called "The Thinking Room,"
  the room where I am sitting.
It has no place to take a bath,
  so "Bathroom" isn't fitting.
I don't see any powder,
  so "The Powder Room" won't fit.
And "Restroom" needs a place to rest;
  the potty isn't it!
So I'll call it "The Thinking Room"
  'cause that is what I do—
I sit and think important thoughts
  while going number two.

My Problem's Worse!

We overslept and missed the bus,
  and everybody's in a fuss.
My Mom's complaining she'll be late;
  she's s'posed to be at work at eight.

And Carla's whining in the back
  that no one packed her morning snack.
And Rudy thinks he's got it rough
  'cause he forgot his science stuff.

But all their problems can't compare—
  at least they're wearing underwear!

Mr. Bear

I'll tell you a story of how old Mr. Bear
Almost went out in his underwear!
Mr. Bear was asleep when he had a bad dream
And woke himself up with a monstrous SCR-E-E-E-A-M!
He was heading outside of his comfortable cave
When I stopped him abruptly to make him behave.

And I said:
"Mr. Bear! Mr. Bear! Now don't you dare
Go out of this cave in your underwear!
Mr. Bear! Mr. Bear! You must be aware
It's winter outside; there's snow in the air!"
He growled at me as if to say,
"Get out of here! Get out of my way!"

But I said:
"Mr. Bear! Mr. Bear! I know it's unfair
To be rudely awakened in a scary nightmare.
But Mr. Bear! Mr. Bear! Please stay right there!
Don't leave your cave! There's snow everywhere!"
He looked at me with eyes half-closed;
Then G-R-O-W-L-E-D again! I nearly froze!

But I said:
"Mr. Bear! Mr. Bear! You'll have to prepare!
A bear mustn't go out in just underwear!
Mr. Bear! Mr. Bear! Sit down in your chair!
If you want to go out, you'll need something to wear!
Let's see, Mr. Bear, here's a coat and a pair
Of boots and hat. . .mmmm, you'll look debonair!
Mr. Bear? Mr. Bear?
Well I do declare!
Mr. Bear is snoring in his underwear!"

Doin' What Mama Says

Mama's always telling us
that brothers need to share.
And Mama's always telling us
to change our underwear.

Tonight we did what Mama says.
And sharing suits us fine!
I'm wearing Jay's used underwear.
And Jay is wearing mine.

Dirty Words

I was making words
    with my alphabet blocks
When my puppy started digging
    in my mommy's flower box.

And my words were getting dirty!
    But my mommy will be glad
That I'm cleaning up my dirty words
    'cause dirty words are bad!

Knight Warning

This is what his mother said
when little Knight went up to bed:

"Get up in the night, My Dear, you must!
Don't wet the bed, or you might rust!"

A Tail-End Tale

Corky stood in line
behind Duffy's behind
and Duffy stood in line behind Boo.

And Boo stood in line
behind Inky's behind
and Inky stood in line behind Drew.

And Drew stood in line
behind Muffy's behind
and Muffy stood in line behind Clown.

And each stood in line
behind the other's behind
till the first one in the line fell down!

What if . . .

At night when I get in my bed,
the "what if's" jump into my head—
What if I get a bad disease?
What if I'm stung by killer bees?
What if I wet my bed at night?
What if I get into a fight?
What if I get an F at school?
What if I drown in Micky's pool?
What if a killer kidnaps me?
What if I couldn't hear or see?
What if my mommy goes away?
What if a monster comes and . . . hey!
Tonight when I get into bed,
I'm gonna think good thoughts instead!

Dimple Wish

I wished I had some dimples
    in my cheeks or in my chin.
Like buttons on a sofa,
    they'd be tucked into my skin.

I thought I'd grow some dimples.
    I figured, in two weeks,
I'd have a nicely-dimpled chin
    and decorated cheeks.

I worked at growing dimples:
    Before I went to sleep,
I poked a finger in my chin,
    a thumbnail in each cheek.

I wish I had some dimples!
    I think it isn't fair!
Some people have deep dimples,
    but my cheeks and chin are bare.

The Thinker

His problem is surely a difficult one!
What CAN he be thinking about?
If I thought for four-hundred years and mor
I think I'd have figured it out.

Is It Fair?

It's not fair!
It isn't!
It's not fair at all!
It's not fair, I tell you!
Just not fair at all
that monkeys
and turkeys
and tigers
and snails
and wombats
and 'possums
and pidgeons have tails.

If I had a tail, I could hang from a tree
and sleep like a sloth, 'stead of sleeping like Me.
If I had a tail, it would make a soft seat;
I'd wag that ol' tail, and I'd get a treat.
If I had a tail, I could chase away flies
and swim a lot faster than people my size.
If I had a tail, I know I could fly
like comets

and rockets—
I'd soar through the sky!
If I had a tail . . .
Well . . . on second thought . . .
If I had a tail, I might get it caught
in car doors
and zippers
and bicycle spokes—
My brothers would tease me and make silly jokes!
And if I had a tail, it'd never be dry—
It'd fall in the toilet
and then . . . I would cry!

So . . . maybe it's right.
I guess it is fair. . .
'Cause a tail'd never fit in a kid's underwear!

Stealing Feelings

When I'm feeling lonely
or frightened
or sad
or angry
or hurt
or guilty
or mad,
The feeling
I'm feeling
begins
as
a
feeling
but
soon
begins
stealing
from all
the good feelings
I had.

Giant Thoughts

If I thought those giants were real,
I'd shiver!
I'd shake!
And I'd squeal!
But I could be wrong, so I'll run along—
Then no one gets me for a meal!

Tooth Truth

I started to think
when I got
a new tooth
that maybe
just maybe
they were telling
the truth.
That maybe
just maybe
I'll get thirty-two,
but now
I have proof!
It cannot be true!

I added a tooth
last Friday
but
then
I lost one today—
I'm subtracting
again!

If the Spider Could Talk

If the spider could talk,
here are words he might say
to the girl who sat eating
her curds and her whey:

Hey, Little Miss Muffet!
Come back to your seat!
I'm only out searching
for insects to eat.

Have you seen any grasshoppers?
Beetles or flies?
I'm looking and looking
with all of my eyes.

Come see my eight legs—
Four pairs to your one.
While your legs have bones,
My whole body has none.

Hey, Little Miss Muffet!
Please don't be afraid.
I'm only a spider.
See the web I have made!

A spider won't bite you
unless it's afraid
or injured somehow.
Gosh! I wish you had stayed!

Hey, Little Miss Muffet!
Look! Your curds and whey
has a fly landing in it—
SLURP!
It's my lucky day!

Willie's House

I like to go to Willie's house.
His momma grabs me and says,
"Howdy, Big Guy! How ya doin'?"
When I grow up, I'm gonna have me
a huggin' house like Willie's.

Solo Sunday

You know the paper,
The one that comes on Sundays,
The big fat one
That takes Dad and Mom all day to read
And leaves me all alone
With no one to talk to me.

Why can't the paper be
Skinny on Sunday
And
Fat on Monday
When I'm in school?

I've Figured It Out

I used to ask where I might go
    to get a dinosaur.
I went to every place in town—
    to every single store.

But all they did was say to me
    (those people in the stores)
"Why, Honey, we sell cats and snakes.
    We don't sell dinosaurs!"

I never ask that question now—
    I've solved it for myself.
I'll never see a dinosaur
    for sale on any shelf!

The reason is (it makes no sense!)
    store owners build their stores
with doors that are too narrow and
    too short for dinosaurs!

Who'll Catch 'Em?

You can catch the chicken pox.
And you can catch the yawn.

        And I will catch the giggles
        and the frisbee on the lawn.

And you can catch the hiccups.
And the robbers.
And the flu.

        And I will catch the movie.
        And the lobster . . . maybe two!

Then you can stop
and catch the breath,

        And I'll go catch the ball.

    And then,
    between the two of us,
    we will have caught 'em all!

Index

Index of First Lines

The Poet Says

A poem is a part of me—
A part of me you cannot see.
You see my head.
You see my hind.
But you can't see what's in my mind.

So I must write that part of me—
The part of me you cannot see.
I take some paper,
A pencil or pen,
To write what's in my mind and then . . .

You have a poem
To read and . . . see!
I've given you a part of me.

Othe... ...ooks by
...wicz